Smelling

by Helen Frost

Consulting Editor: Gail Saunders-Smith, Ph.D.

Consultant: Eric H. Chudler, Ph.D.
Research Associate Professor
Department of Anesthesiology
University of Washington, Seattle

Pebble Books

an imprint of Capstone Press
Mankato, Minnesota

Pebble Books are published by Capstone Press
151 Good Counsel Drive, P.O. Box 669, Mankato, Minnesota 56002
http://www.capstone-press.com

2 3 4 5 6 05 04 03 02 01

Library of Congress Cataloging-in-Publication Data
Frost, Helen, 1949–
Smelling/by Helen Frost.
p. cm.—(The senses)
Includes bibliographical references and index.
Summary: Simple text and photographs present the sense of smell and how
it works.
ISBN 0-7368-0384-X
1. Smell—Juvenile literature. [1. Smell. 2. Senses and sensation.] I. Title.
II. Series: Frost, Helen, 1949– The senses.
QP458.F76   2000
612.8′6—dc21   99-18967
                                                                      CIP

Note to Parents and Teachers

The Senses series supports national science standards for units
related to behavioral science. This book describes and illustrates
the sense of smell. The photographs support early readers in
understanding the text. The repetition of words and phrases helps
early readers learn new words. This book also introduces early
readers to subject-specific vocabulary words, which are defined in
the Words to Know section. Early readers may need assistance to
read some words and to use the Table of Contents, Words to Know,
Read More, Internet Sites, and Index/Word List sections of
the book.

Table of Contents

4

Smell is one of your five senses. You smell with your nose.

Smells are in the air.
You breathe smells
into your nose.

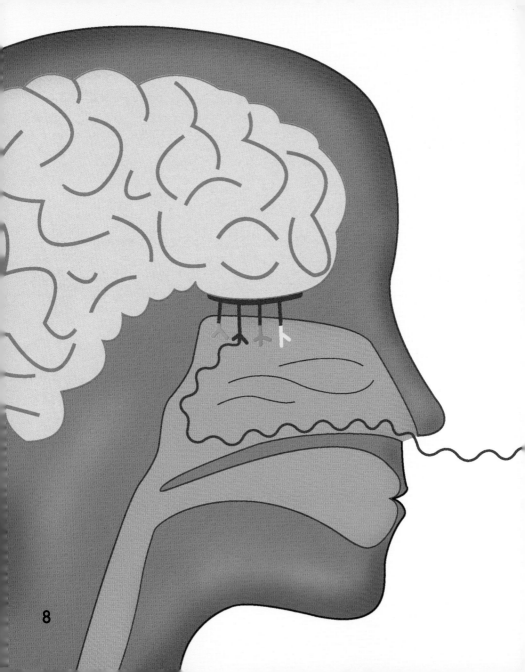

Smell sensors are inside your nose. Different sensors detect different smells.

Some sensors detect the smell of roses.

Some sensors detect
the smell of oranges.

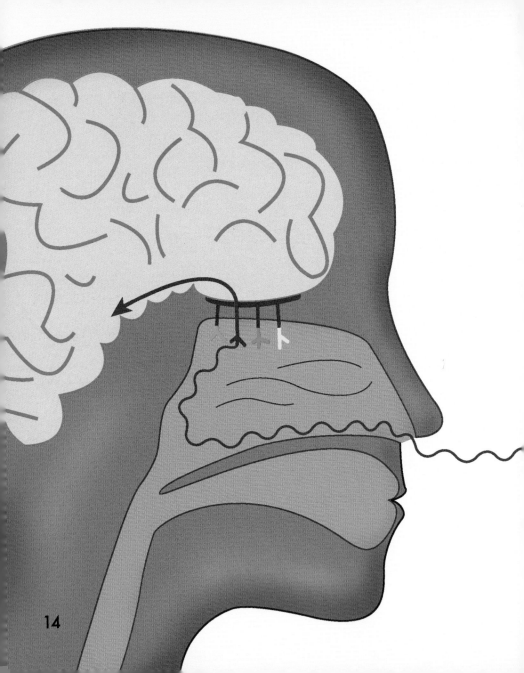

Sensors change smells into signals. The sensors send the signals to your brain.

Your brain understands what you smell. Your brain knows if the smells are good or bad.

Your sense of smell warns you of dangers. It warns you not to eat rotten food.

20

Your sense of smell helps you taste food. The smell of food tells you how it will taste.

Words to Know

brain—the body part inside your head that controls your body; your brain understands what you smell.

detect—to notice something; two olfactory membranes under the bridge of your nose contain sensors that detect different smells.

sense—a way of knowing about things around you; smelling is one of your five senses; hearing, seeing, tasting, and touching are your other senses.

sensor—a cell that detects something about your surroundings; sensors in your nose detect smells.

signal—a message; sensors in your nose send signals to your brain.

taste—to detect the flavor of food and drinks

Read More

Ballard, Carol. *How Do We Taste and Smell?* How Your Body Works. Austin, Texas: Raintree Steck-Vaughn, 1998.

Hurwitz, Sue. *Smell.* The Library of the Five Senses and the Sixth Sense. New York: PowerKids Press, 1997.

Pluckrose, Henry. *Sniffing and Smelling.* Senses. Austin, Texas: Raintree Steck-Vaughn, 1998.

Internet Sites

Smell Experiments
http://facultywashington.edu/chudler/chsmell.html

Your Sense of Smell
http://tqjunior.thinkquest.org/3750/smell/smell.html?tqskip=1

Your Sense of Smell
http://yucky.kids.discovery.com/noflash/body/pg000150html

Index/Word List

Word Count: 111
Early-Intervention Level: 14

Editorial Credits
Mari C. Schuh, editor; Timothy Halldin, cover designer; Kevin T. Kes and
  Linda Clavel, illustrators; Kimberly Danger, photo researcher

Photo Credits
David F. Clobes, 6, 12, 16, 18, 20
Index Stock Imagery/Lynn M. Stone (1992), 10
Jim Cummins/FPG International LLC, 1
Unicorn Stock Photos/Jeff Greenberg, cover; Russell R. Grundke, 4